Festive Flamingo

Written by Shaula Maitland
Illustrated by Kat Stock

For Gerda – A lady who always loved Christmas

Shaula Maitland
www.calmcreatemeditate.com

Illustrated by Kat Stock
www.houseofjack.co.uk

Edited by Rebecca Jensen
www.rebeccaljensen.com

Published by Calm Create Meditate
First Printed: October 2019

ISBN 978-1-9161643-9-0

May meditation bring you many moments of festive calm.

Merry Christmas!

Shaula x

I'm a flamingo who loves to sing,
Have you ever heard such a thing?
When it's Christmas I give a cheer,
As that's my favourite time of year!

Ever since I was very small,
As soon as the snow began to fall,
I would sing my best song,
Yes I really would sing it all day long!

I'd sing on stage, I'd do a jig,
Then I landed my biggest gig.
I was about to perform to the entire flock,
When I had a terrible singing block.

I couldn't remember the merry tune,
It wasn't coming back anytime soon.
My wise friend Panda looked at me,
He said "Meditation is the key."

I sat in silence for many hours,
Hoping to find some superpowers.
Instead I learned to calm my mind,
and my thoughts became much easier to find.

Just when I was about to quit,
Luckily, I remembered it!
I sang and sang all day long,
It truly was my favourite song!

Now I share my flamingo secret with you,
So you can learn to have a calm mind too.
Pick a meditation, any one,
Let's have some FESTIVE FLAMINGO FUN!

Fa la la
la la la la
mingo

Flamingo's Relaxation

Before meditating, try one of these to help you relax.

Christmas Food

Lay your hands out flat to represent a plate. Name a food that you like to eat at Christmas. You may wish to imagine some home baked mince pies, hot Christmas pudding or a delicious roast dinner. Breathe in through your nose smelling the delicious food, pause, and breathe out through your mouth, cooling it down. Repeat for every new food.

Warm Hand

It's cold outside; let's make your hand feel warm and toasty! Close your eyes and hold your hand up to your mouth. Breathe in through your nose and out through your mouth. Take time to feel your breath against your hand, noticing its warmth. Listen carefully to the sound of your breath.

Relaxing by the Fire

Close your eyes. Begin to calm your mind. Feel your breaths going in and out, in and out. Imagine you're seated beside a beautiful, warm fireplace. Sitting on a rug a safe distance away, you watch the orange flames flicker and listen carefully to the crackles and pops. You begin to feel the heat from the fire warming your toes. You begin to feel the warmth rising through your body, relaxing each and every part. Notice your legs - warm and relaxed. Notice your arms - warm and relaxed. Notice your tummy, your shoulders, and your neck - warm and relaxed. You are now warm from the tips of your toes to the very top of your head. Your entire body feels warm and relaxed, peaceful and still.

Snow Boots

Imagine you are getting ready to go outside to play in the snow. You pull up your favourite colourful socks - all the way to your knees. You push your feet down into your welly boots, that have been warming next to the radiator. Feel your feet, warm and cosy. Step outside and watch as your feet disappear into the snow. Push down gently, feeling your feet going deeper and deeper, deeper and deeper into the snow. You feel safe and strong.

Worry Crackers

Close your eyes. Imagine a big tray of worry crackers. They can be any colour you like. Flamingo holds the other end of the cracker. You both pull as hard as you can! With a big POP, the worry disappears! Inside is a tiny message on a rolled up piece of paper. It says, 'Everything is going to be just fine.' Keep popping until all of the crackers have gone. Finally, show us a big SMILE!

Flamingo Hugs

Close your eyes. Imagine Flamingo is giving you the biggest hug. You feel cosy and warm inside Flamingo's feathered wings. Her soft squeeze feels safe and secure. Everything is going to be just fine.

Let's Meditate

Guided visualisations are a simple, yet brilliant way to introduce children to meditation. They capture the imagination, therefore making it easier for children to remain focused and enjoy a moment of calm.

Choosing a meditation

The meditations can be read in any order. You may wish to work through sequentially or pick a page at random. You can revisit the scripts as many times as you like. Each time, children will likely follow new story paths, reflecting their current emotions, experiences and thoughts.

Setting up a calm environment

Meditation can be done anywhere: at home, in the classroom or outside. You just need a quiet space. Playing soft relaxation music can help focus the mind and minimise the effects of background noise. Providing a low light source (such as a candle) acts as a visual cue that relaxation is starting.

Before meditating

It is important to explain to children that if they would like to stop at any time, they can. They just need to wiggle their fingers and open their eyes slowly. If they would prefer to keep their eyes open, encourage them to focus on an object in front of them.

Reading the meditations

Allow children time to imagine the scene by reading slowly in a relaxing voice. When you reach a 'Peace Pause' allow children time to meditate freely, exploring the story in silence. The amount of time required will vary for each individual, but will likely lengthen gradually.

After meditating

Always offer the opportunity for children to share their meditations with you afterwards. Meditation fosters emotive discussion and they are likely to have some exciting stories to tell! To preserve the calm a little longer, children may like to express their meditations through art or writing.

Promoting a positive mindset

Each script nurtures a positive mindset through gently introducing age-appropriate attitudes and skills, such as perseverance, independence and resilience. They also contain a moment of gratitude. Being thankful encourages children to focus on the positive elements of life.

Flamingo symbolism

In meditation, symbolism is very important. Flamingo appears in all twelve meditations for familiarity. She makes the perfect festive meditation companion as she is associated with positivity, vibrancy, confidence and fun!

The Snowflake

Kindness, Individuality and Positive Affirmations

Close your eyes. Imagine you're getting ready to play outside. The mornings are getting chillier by the day. Listen as the zip whooshes up your coat. Feel the soft wool against your forehead as you pull down your hat. Notice the tips of your fingers, all cozy and warm as they plunge into your thick gloves.

But wait - Flamingo doesn't like the cold! What is she going to wear? You rummage around in a large cupboard and pull out every coat imaginable, but none of them fit Flamingo's wide wings.

You have an idea! Taking the blanket from your bed, you carefully drape it over flamingo's wings, covering her like a cape. After adding a colourful clip to hold it in place, Flamingo waddles towards the door, squawking happily.

You dash outside, feeling your legs stretch and your heart pound. It feels amazing to run free. The frosty air touches your cheeks, blows through your hair and fills your lungs. You have never felt more awake. Enjoy running in the garden for a moment, noticing how your body feels.

Peace Pause

With a huge smile, Flamingo falls to the floor and starts making a snow angel. Her feathery wings spread out tall and wide, as she glides them over the snow. In a flash she pops up, revealing a beautiful angel print in the snow.

You decide to make one too. Lying down, you spread your arms tall and begin waving them up and down, from above your head to your sides. Big angel wings begin to appear in the snow. You stretch your legs in and out, in and out, in and out.

Lying there for a moment, you look up at the bright blue sky. There's not a cloud, not a bird, not a plane in sight. The sky is peaceful and still.

Peace Pause

Like a tiny sprinkle of angel dust, one snowflake gently floats down from the sky. It dances in the breeze, swaying from side to side, side to side. You watch it closely as it glitters and twirls, sparkles and whirls. Feel the icy tingle as it lands on your hand. Look closely at its pattern, individual and unique just like you. You thank the sky for the wonderful reminder. I am special. I am unique. I am loved.

Peace Pause

It is now time to come back into the room. You notice the sound of my voice getting louder. You can feel the (chair/bed/floor) beneath you. Wiggle your fingers. Wiggle your toes. Rub your tummy. When you are ready, slowly begin to open your eyes.

Decorating the Tree

Positive Affirmations

Close your eyes. Imagine you're about to decorate the Christmas tree. Flamingo heads into the loft. The old ladder creaks with her every step as she disappears through the dark hatch. After some banging and crashing, the light switch pings and bright white light shines down all around you. You take a few deep breaths in and out, in and out, in and out. You imagine the bright white light filling your entire body, from your toes to your fingertips, all calm and relaxed.

Peace Pause

After searching for a long time, Flamingo finds a big dusty box of decorations. As she climbs down the ladder carrying the box, bells softly jingle inside. Feeling strong, you take the heavy box from Flamingo, placing it gently on the floor. Sparkly tinsel, colourful baubles and delicate bows spill over the sides. Flamingo pulls out a long, knotted string of fairy lights and begins untangling them. It's a big job for Flamingo to do alone. You offer to help. Flamingo is thrilled! Together you unravel the string and begin to decorate the tree.

Peace Pause

It's time to switch on the lights. Flamingo gets ready to press the magic button.

The lights sparkle. A red glow fills the room. I am brave.

The lights glisten. An orange glow fills the room. I am curious.

The lights twinkle. A yellow glow fills the room. I am positive.

Flamingo continues to press the button, watching in amazement. Each time the glow changes, you feel more and more relaxed.

The lights sparkle. A green glow fills the room. I am thankful.
The lights glisten. A blue glow fills the room. I am kind.
The lights twinkle. A purple glow fills the room. I am me!

You stand back and admire the tree. It's magnificent! You thank Flamingo for helping to decorate the tree. You worked brilliantly as a team.

It is now time to come back into the room. You notice the sound of my voice getting louder. You can feel the (chair/bed/floor) beneath you. Wiggle your fingers. Wiggle your toes. Rub your tummy. When you are ready, slowly begin to open your eyes.

Christmas Cards

Choosing Someone Special and Creativity

Close your eyes. Imagine you're about to make a Christmas card for someone special. Spread across the table, there are pots of glitter, bottles of paint, stacks of card and even a few sparkly pompoms. Flamingo dives off into the cupboard and adds a few extra pieces to the table.

Shaking her feathery wings, she begins to create. You join in, selecting a piece of card and picking up a paintbrush. Who would you like to make a card for? Will it be a snowman card, a reindeer card or something else? You choose. Spend some time exploring the materials and making a card for someone special.

Peace Pause

The paint has dried, the glue has stuck and with a few finishing touches, it's time to write inside. You pick up a pen, any colour, and write a message to someone special.

Peace Pause

Placing the card inside an envelope, you carefully write the person's name on the front and Flamingo adds a stamp. Excitedly, you walk up the garden path to a little brown gate. Flamingo swings it open and makes her way up the lane towards the post box. You wait patiently in the garden and watch. Holding the envelope in her beak, she stretches her neck and posts the card. Thankful, you give Flamingo a little clap and she bows happily.

It's time to tidy up! You go back to the table. There's paint, glitter and sparkly pompoms everywhere! You start putting away the art materials while Flamingo goes to the sink for a wet cloth. You both work together to get the job done.

Peace Pause

As you place the last pompom back in the craft box, you hear a cheeky giggle from under the table. Crouching down, you see Flamingo with a bright red pompom at the end of her beak; she's pretending to be a reindeer. Funny Flamingo!

It is now time to come back into the room. You notice the sound of my voice getting louder. You can feel the (chair/bed/floor) beneath you. Wiggle your fingers. Wiggle your toes. Rub your tummy. When you are ready, slowly begin to open your eyes.

Snow Day

Feeling in Control, Making Choices and Investigating ideas

Close your eyes. Imagine you're in the garden. The sun is shining, the sky is blue and the ground is covered with fresh white snow. A little robin lands gently on a branch of a nearby tree. He twitters loudly, pushing out his large red tummy. A white feather softly falls from the sky. You watch as it gently sways from side to side, getting closer and closer, closer and closer. You reach up as high as you possibly can, stretching up onto tip-toes. The feather gently falls into your hand. Tickle your hand with it for a moment. How do you feel as you hold this feather?

Peace Pause

You offer the feather to Robin. He jumps down and rests on your fingertips, taking the feather carefully in his beak. He's so thankful; it will be brilliant for his nest. He twitters loudly, ruffles his wings and flies away.

Flamingo calls from behind you. She's come to play. She waddles through the snow wearing giant welly boots and dragging a sledge behind her. Together you climb up a slope in the garden. Once you reach the very top, Flamingo puts the sledge down so you can have a closer look.

Would you like to sledge down the hill? You can have a go or you can watch Flamingo, it's up to you. Perhaps you could ride with Flamingo. This sledge is magic. It can go as fast or as slow as you'd like. It can even stop if you ask it to. You are in control. You are very safe. Spend some time enjoying the snow.

Peace Pause

Flamingo makes a snowball with her wings and rolls it down the slide. What a great idea! You decide to play a game, who can roll their snowball the furthest? Ready, steady… hey, Flamingo let go too soon! Watch as the snowball tumbles down the icy track. You both laugh and try again. You win, then Flamingo wins; it's all good fun! With lots of questions, you start to experiment. Do bigger snowballs roll further? Are there any other places in the garden to roll snowballs?

Peace Pause

Your hands begin to get a little chilly. It's time to go inside to warm up. You trudge through the soft snow back to the door. As you pull off your wellies and stand them neatly on the mat, you listen closely to bells playing softly in the distance. Their happy tune fills your heart and makes you smile. Sitting on the mat for a moment, you watch the garden calm and still.

It is now time to come back into the room. You notice the sound of my voice getting louder. You can feel the (chair/bed/floor) beneath you. Wiggle your fingers. Wiggle your toes. Rub your tummy. When you are ready, slowly begin to open your eyes.

Feeding the Birds

Generosity, Kindness and Caring for Nature

Close your eyes. Imagine you're walking through the woods. You can hear the crispy, brown leaves crunch beneath your feet, while the branches sway gently in the breeze. The squirrels are running up and down the trees, the birds are searching for berries and the badgers are tucked up asleep in their dens.

Holding a bird book, you look up into the trees trying to spot each type. Flamingo is looking closely through her binoculars, squawking wildly. Perched quietly on a holly branch is a little brown bird with a red tummy. Flamingo waves the tip of her wing over the pages. It's a robin! You stand quietly, gazing around the wood, watching the birds.

Peace Pause

After watching the birds for some time, you decide you'd like to make them a feeder. It can be tricky for birds to find food in the winter. You begin searching the woodland floor for pine cones. The bigger the better! Flamingo opens her backpack and places it on the floor ready to fill. Spend some time collecting pine cones.

Peace Pause

Flamingo comes out from a bush holding a wingful of pine cones. You buckle up the bag and swing it onto your back. Feel the weight on your shoulders, the straps pressing down firmly. Take a deep breath in and out, in and out.

It's time to go home. You stomp through the wood, crunch, crunch, crunch, crunch. You glide through the long grass, swish, swish, swish, swish. You slide through the mud, squelch, squelch, squelch, squelch. You run over the wooden bridge, thud, thud, thud, thud. You open the squeaky gate, creak, creak, creak, creak. You tiptoe down the path, patter, patter, patter, patter, all the way home.

After taking off your coat and boots, you sit at the table, ready to begin. Flamingo fetches a large mixing bowl, some melted lard and a huge bag of bird seed. You mix the ingredients together and press the sticky bird food onto the pine cone, covering each and every spike. Flamingo adds the string, tying it carefully with her beak. You place it the fridge to set. While you wait, you spend time with Flamingo, chatting and playing.

Peace Pause

Once the feeders are ready to hang, you make your way into the garden. You may want to hang your feeders on the fence, a low branch or somewhere else - you choose. Flamingo stretches her long neck and hangs hers from the treehouse. Robin twitters and happily flaps your way, tucking into your delicious treat. Seeing Robin eating the food you prepared makes you feel happy. It's feels good to give to others.

It is now time to come back into the room. You notice the sound of my voice getting louder. You can feel the (chair/bed/floor) beneath you. Wiggle your fingers. Wiggle your toes. Rub your tummy. When you are ready, slowly begin to open your eyes.

A Christmas Recipe

Resilience, Perseverance and Creativity

Close your eyes. Imagine you're in the kitchen, sitting at a small table. A bright, colourful tablecloth is carefully placed over it, ready for cooking. You go to the sink to wash your hands, stepping up on a little stool so you can reach. You turn on the tap and hold your hands underneath the warm running water. Feel as the water glides over your fingertips. Feel any worries disappear, flowing out and away, out and away. Adding some soap, you rub your hands together to make lots of bubbles. Watch closely as they pop one by one, one by one. With one last rinse, Flamingo passes you a towel to dry your hands. Take your time. Feel the towel, fluffy and soft. With one last pat you're ready to begin. It's time to bake!

You reach for the recipe book. It's at the top of the bookshelf. You stretch and stretch. Growing a little taller on tip-toes, you finally manage to get it down. The Christmas recipe book only comes down once a year. You flick through the dusty pages. Gingerbread, Cookies, Biscuits... Ah-ha! That's the one!

You rummage around the cupboards, selecting all of the necessary ingredients and neatly arrange them on the table. One spoon of sugar... One cup of flour... Yes it's all here!

You put the ingredients into a large bowl and look for the wooden spoon. Where is it? It's missing. You look under the table - not there! You look under your chair - not there either! You look across the kitchen to see Flamingo dancing in her apron, singing into a wooden spoon as if it was a microphone! There it is! Flamingo giggles and passes it back.

You begin to mix the ingredients together, stirring round and round, round and round. After lots of mixing, the dough is ready. Like a big ball of playdough, you can roll it and squash it, pull it and twist it, pat it and cut it.

Flamingo comes to the table with a large box of cookie cutters. You can make anything you like: a house; a dinosaur; an igloo. Anything at all! You begin building your biscuit shape, one small piece at a time. Watch as a masterpiece begins to appear, so detailed, so real. You prod and nudge until every last detail is finished. Take a moment to explore all of its possibilities.

Peace Pause

You carefully transfer your finished model to a baking tray. Uh-oh, the tray wobbles! Uh-oh, the model shakes! Uh-oh, a big piece falls off! It's ok, you can handle this, it won't take long to fix. You build the model again, making it even better than it was before.

Impressed, Flamingo takes it to the oven. The yummy smell of baking fills the air, while you sit patiently listening to the clock, tick-tock, tick-tock, tick-tock. After waiting for what feels like forever, you hear the ding of a timer and peek through the glass. It looks tasty! Flamingo protects her feathery wings and carefully pulls out the hot tray. It looks delicious. After waiting for it to cool, you both take a bite. It tastes delicious too!

It is now time to come back into the room. You notice the sound of my voice getting louder. You can feel the (chair/bed/floor) beneath you. Wiggle your fingers. Wiggle your toes. Rub your tummy. When you are ready, slowly begin to open your eyes.

Woodland Ice-skating

Independence, Perseverance and Self-Belief

Close your eyes. Imagine you're walking through the woods. It's a beautiful sunny day. Snow covers the ground; icicles hang from the trees, and the soft sound of bells gently rings in the distance. You're going to go ice-skating! There's a special ice-rink in the middle of the woods. It's used by the woodland animals. Flamingo is going to meet you there.

You weave through the old trees, gliding your hands over their rough bark. Every tree you touch makes you feel stronger and stronger, stronger and stronger. The sun is shining through the leaves above; creating wonderful shadows on the snow. You stop for a moment, looking at the beautiful patterns.

Peace Pause

You come to the edge of the forest and can see the ice rink in the valley below. Thrilled to be wearing your waterproofs, you slide down the hill, roll down the hill, run down the hill, it's entirely up to you.

Flamingo waits with a round of applause. She holds out your skates. Thanking her, you take the skates and begin putting them on. What do they look like? Are they colourful? Do they have pictures on them?

You stand at the side and watch the other skaters. Mole is twirling, Badger is racing and Rabbit is jumping with style. Flamingo takes your hand and guides you onto the ice. You stumble a little. You haven't been ice-skating before. Flamingo doesn't let go, she helps you to become steady on your feet. You feel safe. You feel confident. You'd like to have a go on your own. After a few wobbles, you begin to get the hang of it. You glide around the rink all on your own. You're getting good at this! Well done! Enjoy some time skating on the ice with Flamingo and her friends.

Peace Pause

You were brilliant! You didn't let a stumble stop you; you kept learning and improving. It was very brave to ice-skate on your own. You suddenly feel very proud.

Flamingo skates over and lays her wings flat offering you a gift. You gently move her feathers aside to reveal the most beautiful snow globe. Taking a closer look, you notice that this is a very special snow globe, not like any other. Inside is a tiny figure of you and Flamingo ice-skating with your new friends. You give it a shake and glittery snow fills the globe. You watch as the snow slowly begins to settle. You thank Flamingo for the wonderful memories. The perfect end to the perfect day! One that you will always remember!

It is now time to come back into the room. You notice the sound of my voice getting louder. You can feel the (chair/bed/floor) beneath you. Wiggle your fingers. Wiggle your toes. Rub your tummy. When you are ready, slowly begin to open your eyes.

Snow Camel

Adventure, Choices and Teamwork

Close your eyes. Imagine you've just stepped out into a snowy garden. The lawn is white, the trees are white, even the top of the trampoline is white. Listen to the sound of the snow crunching beneath your feet as you walk. Watch as you leave a trail of glistening footprints behind you. Glide your glove over the frozen water in the fountain and the icicles hanging from the slide.

Flamingo comes out of the house wearing a crown and a cloak; she's dressed up as a wise man! She skips over merrily, pretending to ride a camel and passes you a costume. You look at the crown carefully. What colour are the jewels? What shape? What size? Placing the crown on your head, you suddenly feel very wise indeed. So wise in fact, you have a brilliant idea! Let's make a snow camel!

Flamingo jumps up ready to build. But how will you make one? Working together, you begin to roll a ball of snow around the garden, watching it get bigger and bigger, bigger and bigger. That's the body. You carry on building; rolling a head and four long legs. How many humps will the camel have? Enjoy spending some time with Flamingo building your snow camel.

Peace Pause

Now, you just need a few finishing touches. Perhaps some long twigs for the eyelashes, some large black buttons for the eyes and some small white pebbles for the teeth. Feeling proud, you stand back and admire your camel for a moment.

Flamingo flaps her wings and a magical bright white light shines. It feels fresh. It feels new. It feels exciting! As the white glow disappears, you hear hooves patter. Your camel is alive!

Camel shivers; it's very cold outside. Flamingo kindly drapes a scarf around his neck, while you excitedly introduce yourself. Camel is very friendly, very kind and very wise. You can ask him anything and he'll try to help. You can choose to talk to Camel or go for a ride. He will always keep you safe. You can go anywhere you like, anywhere at all.

Peace Pause

The sun is now setting in the sky, and the moon begins to rise. Day turns to night. Twinkling stars fill the sky. What a beautiful sight! It's time to say goodbye. You thank Camel for a lovely day. He smiles and nods, as he disappears through the snow, following a star. I guess it's what Christmas camels were made to do.

It is now time to come back into the room. You notice the sound of my voice getting louder. You can feel the (chair/bed/floor) beneath you. Wiggle your fingers. Wiggle your toes. Rub your tummy. When you are ready, slowly begin to open your eyes.

The Lost Tail

Courage, Acceptance, Disappointment and Self-Belief

Close your eyes. Imagine you're a sheep in the Christmas play. Feel your wooly costume, all cuddly and soft. You're lovely and warm; it's the best costume for a cold winter's day. You hear Flamingo call you over to have your face painted. You join the queue patiently behind two angels, and after a few minutes, it's your turn! Sitting down in the chair, you notice an amazing array of colour on the table next to you. There's glitter, paints, sponges and brushes. Flamingo squawks excitedly. Picking up a sponge, she lightly dabs your face white. Feel the sponge against your cheeks, noticing every touch. Feel the brush tickle the end of your nose. Flamingo flaps her wings. You're finished and ready for the show.

Walking past a mirror, you catch a glance at your face. It's incredible; you look just like a sheep! Flamingo has done a fantastic job. You reach up and feel your little sheep ears, neatly positioned on a headband. While checking your costume in the mirror, you notice a tiny tag hanging out from your sock. Flamingo carefully nibbles at it with her beak and, with one small tug, it's gone. There - all done!

But wait! Where's your tail? You begin searching inside your bag, under the chair and around the classroom. It's nowhere to be seen! Spend some time looking for your tail.

Peace Pause

You've spent a long time looking, but the tail is still nowhere to be seen! You are being called to line up, the show is about to begin! It can feel disappointing when you lose something or things don't work out how you planned. Today you lost your tail, but you can still take part in the show. You take a deep breath and let go of any worry or nerves. You repeat - I can... I can... I can and I will. You walk confidently up to the line and wait for a signal.

You hear the music start - that's your cue. You bound on stage. The lights shine so bright, but you can just make out the people you love watching in the audience. They're cheering and waving, they're so proud of you. YOU feel proud of you! You sing, you dance and when it's your moment to shine, you let out the biggest "Baaaaa" yet! What a fantastic performance. Happily take a bow and enjoy your moment in the spotlight.

It's time to go backstage. Flamingo is waiting for you. She's so happy that you went ahead with the show even though you lost your tail. That was very brave; it took courage. Flamingo ruffles her feathers and pulls out... the tail! Where had it been? Flamingo points to the top of the Christmas tree! How did it get there? You thank Flamingo for finding it, as she carefully pins it to the back of your costume ready for next year.

It is now time to come back into the room. You notice the sound of my voice getting louder. You can feel the (chair/bed/floor) beneath you. Wiggle your fingers. Wiggle your toes. Rub your tummy. When you are ready, slowly begin to open your eyes.

Toy Workshop

Creativity, Generosity and Taking Turns

Close your eyes. Imagine you're in Santa's workshop. The elves are busy making toys for the special day. You can hear hammers tapping, scissors cutting and drills whirring. All the elves have a job. All the elves know what to do. All the elves are busy. You decide to wander around the workshop quietly to have a closer look.

Peace Pause

As you crawl through a tiny door, you're welcomed by Flamingo. She is surrounded by pens, paint and big sheets of paper. She flaps her feathery wings, pleased to see you! She needs your help. Flamingo would like to make a game for the elves. What a wonderful idea! You sit down beside her and begin drawing a big track, while Flamingo dabs dots onto some little wooden dice. Is your game going to have question cards, special instructions or tokens to collect? You listen carefully to each other's ideas, working together to make an incredible game.

Peace Pause

You've worked together brilliantly. It can be tricky when you have different ideas, but you chose to compromise. You listened to each other and picked the best ideas, sometimes mixing them up to create even better ideas!

The game looks wonderful! You can't wait to play it! You roll the dice and move your counter forward, counting the spaces. Flamingo takes her turn. You carry on playing, taking turns and having fun.

Peace Pause

It's time to put the game in a box for the elves. You write a little note explaining how to play and place it inside. Flamingo wraps it up in an instant. How did she manage that? The silky smooth ribbon gently curls down the side of the box.

In the corner of the room is a parcel slide. It's used to send presents around the workshop. You place the present on the slide and push gently, watching it disappear. You rush to the window, looking down at the elves working below. Your present flies into a big collection bag. An elf picks it up and he looks confused. He jumps up and down with excitement. No-one has ever made the elves a present before! Word spreads quickly as the elves gather to play the game. A warm, fuzzy feeling grows inside you. It feels good to see others happy.

It is now time to come back into the room. You notice the sound of my voice getting louder. You can feel the (chair/bed/floor) beneath you. Wiggle your fingers. Wiggle your toes. Rub your tummy. When you are ready, slowly begin to open your eyes.

Reindeer's Stable

Friendship

Close your eyes. Imagine you're on Reindeer's back, riding through the frozen Arctic. Flamingo's wings are wrapped tightly around your waist as she sits quietly behind you. Feel Reindeer's fur between your fingers, warm and soft. Feel her antlers, tall and smooth. Feel her heartbeat, steady and strong. You journey through the frozen arctic with two wonderful friends. Reindeer's hooves leave a long trail of prints in the fresh snow behind you. With each step you feel more and more relaxed.

Peace Pause

The stars are twinkling. The moon shines bright. You look up and admire the night sky, so beautiful, so peaceful, so still. Tonight feels special.

Flamingo lifts her wing and points. You see smoke coming from a chimney far away in the distance. As you ride closer, you begin to see a little more. The little wooden house has a pointy roof covered in snow, candles flicker in the windows and a wreath hangs perfectly on a little red door. A stable sits to the side of the house, it's Reindeer's home. Reindeer snuffles with excitement and plods on.

As you reach the big doors of the stable, Reindeer bends, allowing you and Flamingo to jump down. You slowly lift the latch and go inside. The stable is warm and dimly lit. Reindeer lies down on a bed of straw, curling up after her long walk in the snow. You and Flamingo rest beside her, nestling into her warm fur. As you lay back, looking up at the roof above, you notice a tiny family of mice sitting on the beam. They are all wearing tiny woolen hats and are singing your favourite Christmas song. Lie back on Reindeer's warm fur and enjoy the show.

Peace Pause

You give the mice a round of applause. They curtsey and bow politely; blowing air kisses to the audience. Glitter falls from the ceiling. What a fabulous show! Flamingo is very impressed!

The door creeks and in comes an elf, holding a tray of cookies, carrots, shrimp and a warm glass of milk. He sits down beside you, offering a tasty snack. The cookies smell delicious, homemade and warm from the oven. Thanking him politely, you take a glass of milk and sip through the paper straw. Reindeer munches happily on a carrot, while Flamingo tucks into the shrimp. It is the perfect end, to the perfect day!

It is now time to come back into the room. You notice the sound of my voice getting louder. You can feel the (chair/bed/floor) beneath you. Wiggle your fingers. Wiggle your toes. Rub your tummy. When you are ready, slowly begin to open your eyes.

Christmas Eve

Communication, Curiosity and Kindness

Close your eyes. Imagine it's Christmas Eve. Before going to bed, you prepare a special snack. First you head into the fridge. The light comes on, shining a warm glow all around you. The frosty chill touches your arm as you reach for the milk. Pouring it carefully into a glass carefully, you watch as a few bubbles pop. Adding a red and white stripy straw to the glass, you place it neatly on a special tray. Father Christmas might get thirsty on his busy trip tonight.

Next you delve into a big bag of carrots, looking for the biggest, juiciest one for the reindeer. Once you've made your choice, you place it onto the tray next to the milk. There's just one thing left to find.

Flamingo has baked some mince pies especially for tonight. She carefully takes them out of the oven, placing them on the side. They smell delicious! They're all different shapes and sizes. You think carefully. Which one would Father Christmas like? Picking your favourite, you place it gently on the tray.

Deciding to write a note, you sit down with a pencil and a small piece of paper. You may want to ask Father Christmas question. How many reindeers does he have? How long did it take the elves to make all of the presents? Where's his favourite place to visit?

Peace Pause

You say goodnight and head to bed. You've had a very busy day. Tucked up in bed, you think of all the wonderful moments tomorrow will bring. You notice the fresh smell of the pillow, cold against your cheek. The soft duvet, warming up from head to toe, making you feel more and more relaxed.

You listen carefully, enjoying a moment of calm. The house is quiet and still. Everyone is asleep. That's when you notice the faint sound of bells jingling in the distance. Could that be the sleigh? Next you hear the crunch of a carrot. Could that be the reindeer?

You poke a toe out from the warm covers. Brrr! It's chilly! You get out of bed, wrapping your dressing gown tightly around you. Feel the cold floor beneath your feet. You creep down the stairs, one by one. You can hear Flamingo snoring loudly. The stairs creek, you tread slowly. Flamingo wakes up, yawns and stretches her wings.

You both go to the window, taking a peek outside. The moon is shining, the stars are twinkling and the snow sparkles on the lawn. Not a sleigh in sight.

Turning around, you notice the tray. The milk is half drunk, the mince pie half eaten and the carrot completely gone. A tiny note rests beside the tray. A note just for you! Take a moment to read it carefully. Enjoy your special letter from Father Christmas.

Peace Pause

It is now time to come back into the room. You notice the sound of my voice getting louder. You can feel the (chair/bed/floor) beneath you. Wiggle your fingers. Wiggle your toes. Rub your tummy. When you are ready, slowly begin to open your eyes.

More Friends to Meet...

Panda explains how to meditate with a short rhyming story. She begins relaxation with simple breathing exercises and visualisations, before sharing twelve inspiring and uplifting meditations. Each one focusing on positive attributes such as self-belief, perseverance, independence and curiosity.

Enjoy the benefits of meditation with journeys that spark the imagination. Explore the delights of 'Mermaid Cave', feast on a delicious 'Midnight Picnic' and discover what is inside the mysterious 'Green Egg'.

48712019R00023

Printed in Poland
by Amazon Fulfillment
Poland Sp. z o.o., Wrocław